# Buildings, Buildings, Buildings

**Judith Bauer Stamper**

**Teaching**Strategies™ • Washington D.C.

**Copyright © 2010 by Teaching Strategies, Inc.**

All rights reserved. No part of this publication may be reproduced or distributed in any form, or by any means, or stored in a database or retrieval system without the prior written permission of Teaching Strategies, Inc.

For Teaching Strategies, Inc.
Publisher: Larry Bram
Editorial Director: Hilary Parrish Nelson
VP Curriculum and Assessment: Cate Heroman
Product Manager: Kai-leé Berke
Book Development Team: Sherrie Rudick and Jan Greenberg
Project Manager: Jo A. Wilson

For Q2AMedia
Editorial Director: Bonnie Dobkin
Editor and Curriculum Adviser: Suzanne Barchers
Program Manager: Gayatri Singh
Creative Director: Simmi Sikka
Project Manager: Santosh Vasudevan
Designers: Shruti Aggarwal & Ritu Chopra
Picture Researcher: Stephanie Mills

Picture Credits
t-top b-bottom c-center l-left r-right

Cover: Kathleen & Scott Snowden/Istockphoto, Sascha Burkard/Dreamstime, Visions LLC/Photolibrary, Dennis Morris/Istockphoto.

Back Cover: FloridaStock/Shutterstock, Paul Yates/Shutterstock, Kenneth C. Zirkel/Istockphoto.

Title page: The Solomon R. Guggenheim Museum, New York/Goodshoot/Photolibrary.

Insides: PhotostoGo: 3, Judy Glick-Smith: 4, Thinkstock/Jupiter Images: 5, Dennis Morris/Istockphoto: 6, Andersen Ross/Photolibrary: 7, Judy Glick-Smith: 8, PhotostoGo: 9, Jon Patton/Istockphoto: 10, prism66/Shutterstock: 11, Kathleen & Scott Snowden/Istockphoto: 12, Photolibrary: 13, Judy Glick-Smith: 14, Judy Glick-Smith: 15, Frank Chmura/Photolibrary: 16, Paul Prescott/Shutterstock: 17, Visions LLC/Photolibrary: 18, Scott Boehm/Getty Images: 19, The Solomon R. Guggenheim Museum, New York/Goodshoot/Photolibrary: 20, The Solomon R. Guggenheim Museum, New York/Pepeira Tom/Photolibrary: 21, Sascha Burkard/Dreamstime: 22, Van Hart/Shutterstock: 23, FloridaStock/Shutterstock: 24l, Paul Yates/Shutterstock: 24tr, Kenneth C. Zirkel/Istockphoto: 24br.

Teaching Strategies, Inc.
P.O. Box 42243
Washington, DC 20015
www.TeachingStrategies.com

Library of Congress Cataloging-in-Publication Data
Stamper, Judith Bauer.
  Buildings, buildings, buildings / Judith Bauer Stamper.
    p. cm.
  ISBN 978-1-60617-140-0
  1. Buildings--Juvenile literature. I. Title.
  TH149.S73 2010
  720--dc22
                              2009036545

ISBN: 978-1-60617-140-0

CPSIA tracking label information:
RR Donnelley, Shenzhen, China
Date of Production: April 2014
Cohort: Batch 4

Printed and bound in China

| 6 7 8 9 10 | 15 14 |
|------------|-------|
| Printing | Year Printed |

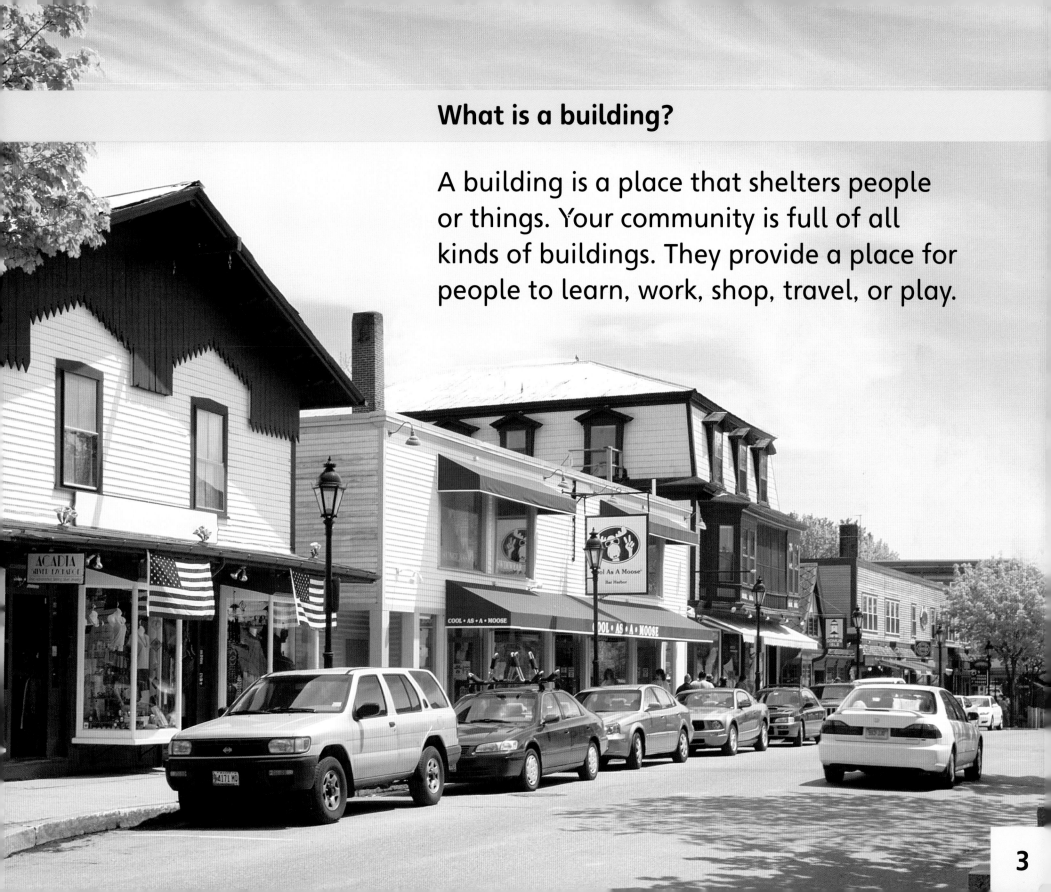

## What is a building?

A building is a place that shelters people or things. Your community is full of all kinds of buildings. They provide a place for people to learn, work, shop, travel, or play.

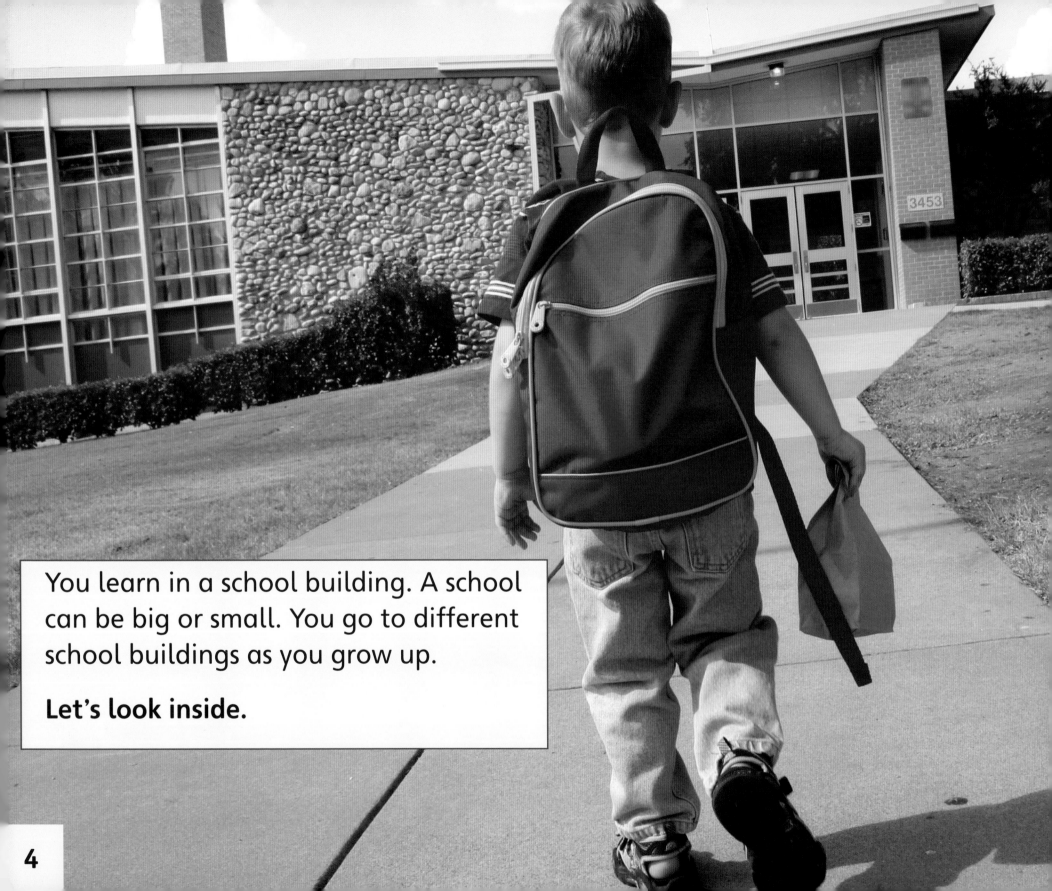

You learn in a school building. A school can be big or small. You go to different school buildings as you grow up.

**Let's look inside.**

Inside a school.

Libraries are built for learning, too. One thing all libraries have in common is lots of books.

**Let's look inside.**

Inside a library.

You can shop for food in a grocery store. A grocery store can be a little shop on the corner or a huge supermarket.

**Let's look inside.**

Inside a supermarket.

A post office is a building where workers send mail all over the country and the world. Big post offices in large cities handle millions of pieces of mail each year. Even a small-town post office handles mail in large numbers!

**Let's look inside.**

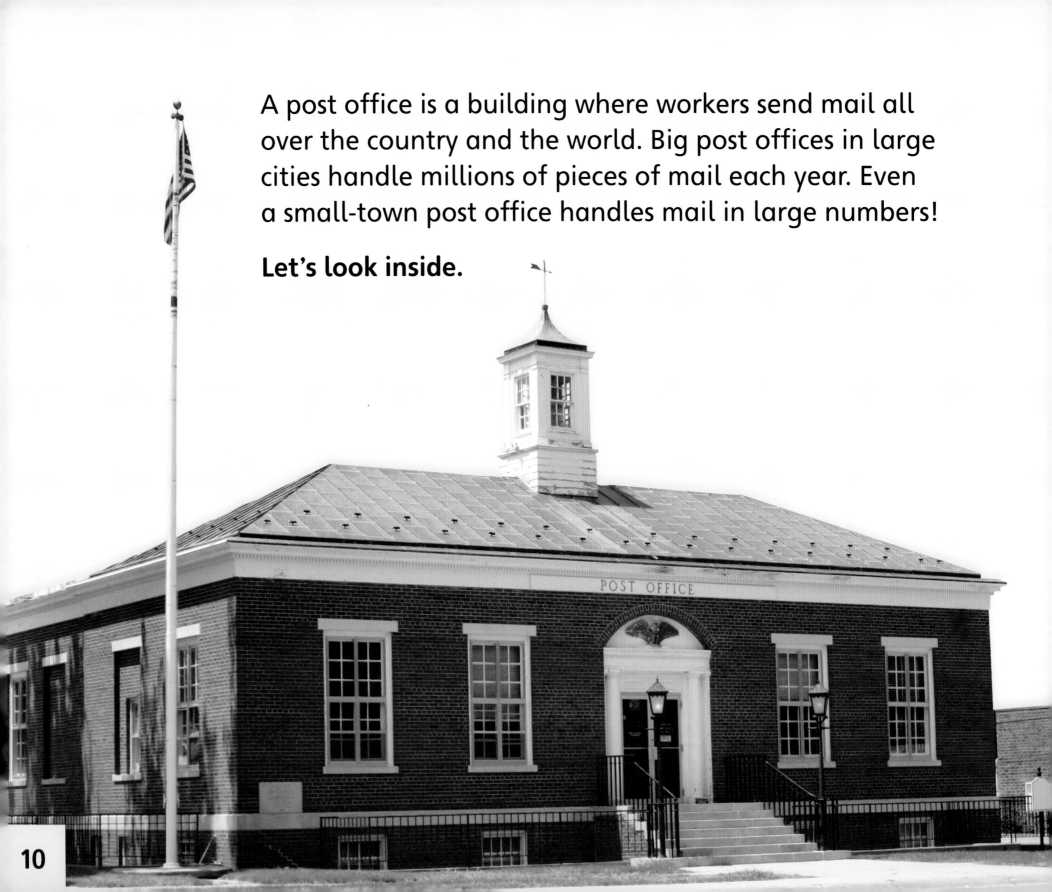

POST OFFICE

Inside a post office.

Hospitals are buildings where doctors and nurses work. Hospitals have patient rooms, operating rooms, recovery rooms, and rooms full of special equipment for saving lives and treating diseases.

**Let's look inside.**

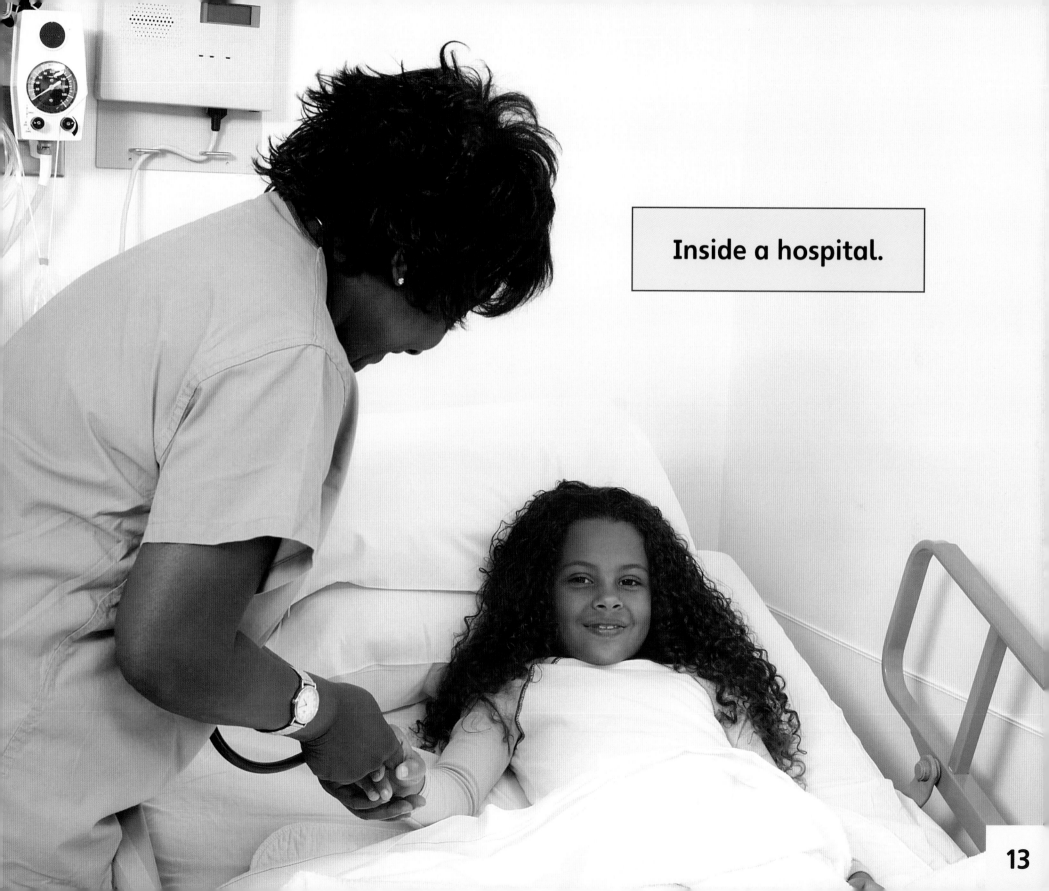

Inside a hospital.

Adults go to work in many different types of buildings. A huge office building has many small offices inside. A factory has large rooms with machines. Factories make everything from cars to toys.

**Let's look inside.**

Inside a car factory.

There are special buildings where journeys start and end. At an airport, passengers get on and off planes at big buildings called terminals. Trains and ships have terminals, too.

**Let's look inside.**

Inside an airport.

Do you like sports? Millions of people do! Cheering fans pack basketball arenas, ballparks, and football stadiums.

**Let's look inside.**

Inside a football stadium.

Some buildings were made for sharing beautiful
art and music. People hear music in concert halls.
They look at art in art museums.
The buildings can be beautiful, too.

**Let's look inside.**

GUGGENHEIM MUSEUM

Inside a museum.

Our country celebrates its history and heroes with buildings that are monuments and memorials. The Lincoln Memorial in Washington, D.C., honors President Abraham Lincoln.

**Let's look inside.**

Inside the
Lincoln Memorial.

Every building has a special job.
**Can you guess what these buildings do?**